Soul
Notes Too

♬ ♬

poems from the heart, mind,
and pen
of

Minx Boren

Let your soul sing

Minx

Soul Notes Too
ISBN 0-9702550-1-2
© 2003 by Minx Boren

Published by:
Fourfold Path Inc.
PO Box 30843
Palm Beach Gardens,
FL 33420-0843
email: Minx@CoachMinx.com

First Printing: July, 2003

Printed in the United States of America

On the cover:
"Friends"
acrylic on canvas by Patti Burris
© 1988 Patti Burris
all rights reserved

Copies of <u>Soul Notes</u> and <u>Soul Notes Too</u> may be obtained by contacting Fourfold Path Inc. by e-mail or regular mail at the above address.

♪ ♫ ♪ ♫ ♪ ♫ ♪ ♫

Dedication

To each of you who, no matter what,
is courageous enough... and willing...
to connect with me
again and again
at the level of our souls.

You know who you are.

Namaste

About the Cover

Artist Patti Burris
"Friends"
acrylic on canvas 4' x 4'

Patti Burris is a professional artist and teacher with more than 35 years of experience. Her paintings have been exhibited and collected nationally. She lives in Santa Monica, CA and teaches at the Brentwood Art Center. Her painting "Inner Reflections" appeared on the cover of my first book, <u>Soul Notes</u>. I purchased "Friends" from Patti almost 15 years ago and it has hung in my home ever since. I am delighted to now have it grace the cover of this book.

""For me, the essence of life is about relationships and touching lives. 'Friends' was created as the cornerstone of a one woman exhibit on the theme of the qualities of friendship - intimacy, tenderness, acceptance, loyalty, love, trust, and respect. Like the poems in this book, my paintings are about those precious and connecting moments when we embrace life fully. As always, the common thread that weaves itself through my work is a positive affirmation of life." P.B.

Preface

*"Integrity is the acceptance of
everything we have done."*
≈ Julio Olalla

...and said and been and thought. Owning it
all. Writing poetry does that. It forces integrity
and demands authenticity. Without either there
can be no substance, no vibrancy, no life. Each
time I write, I have the feeling I am exposing
myself in some daring and provocative way. Of
course, there are times when I would prefer to hide
behind prettier phrases and easier revelations.
But then the words simply do not ring true.
And since "beauty is truth and truth beauty..."

While gathering the poems for this collection I
realized that they seemed to reflect the basic
theme of attending to the precious moments of
our lives, both alone and in connection, and so I
have chosen to group them accordingly. Of
course you, dear reader, are free to peruse the
contents randomly if you prefer. Either way,
my prayer is that you enjoy your meanderings.

M.B.
Palm Beach Gardens, FL
July 13th, 2003

"The soul is not a thing.
It is a place from which to
speak."

≈ Julio Olalla

♪ ♫ ♪ ♫ ♪ ♫ ♪ ♫

THE GIFT OF A POEM

I do not understand
the urge that pushes
up and through my
busyness
at odd times and
places causing me to
abandon all semblance
of plan and
to grab my pen in
response to some inner
voice

what muse
whispers sweet
somethings and
how do I hear them
above
and beyond the din
of all that vies for
my attention
on an ordinary day
like today

there is it seems
an infinity of
inspiration always
hovering about
while periodically I
am moved to
allow words to tumble
onto the page
in an order of their
own choosing
as I play
dutiful scribe to
some inner mistress

⌘ ⌘ ⌘ ⌘ ⌘ ⌘

Precious Moments

"The aim of life is to live, and to live means to be aware, joyously, drunkenly, serenely, divinely aware."

Henry Miller

there is a silence
that is heavy
burdensome
of unshed tears
and words unspoken
of song's unsung
and never were's
or will be's

there is a silence
that is electric
exciting
of breath held
in anticipation
and body tensed
in preparation
for some great
and magnificent effort

there is a silence
that is weighty
significant
of waiting for
the verdict
or outcome
that could change
everything
or nothing

there is a silence
that is reverent
awe-filled
of the moments before
the sun's rising
or a baby's first cry
or when we are held
enthralled by the grace
and power of
an eagle's flight

there are so very many
qualities of silence
each one holy
shhhhhhhh
are you listening
to the spaces
between the notes?

⌘ ⌘ ⌘ ⌘ ⌘ ⌘

minutes, hours, days
my most precious wealth
like golden coins
jingling in my pocket
awaken me
from time to time
to the present moment
as a dharma bell
reminding me that
they are here
to be spent
but not wasted

sometimes I am miserly
counting out
these timely tokens
ever so carefully
in the day runner
that would run my days
other times
I judiciously offer
the greater portion
of my riches
with discretionary beneficence
generously
measuring and doling
pleased with the worthiness
of my selections

but of course
there are those times
of frivolous abandon
when the minutes
pour out everywhere
in gay profusion
gracing the palms
of friends and strangers alike
as I allow myself
to be enticed and enthused
by the variety
of life's grand bazaar
uncontainable
purse strings slackened
sufficiently loosed
by my passion
beyond the constraints
of my practicality

it's true of course
these very moments
are the richest of all
wildly serendipitous time
out of time
replenishing my life
adding immeasurable value
to each precious coin
lavishly dispensed
in the feeding of my soul
⌘ ⌘ ⌘ ⌘ ⌘ ⌘

it was
an unencumbered moment
soft and light filled
gone
were the fears and frustrations
vanished
the judgments
the anger
no interfering static
no sadness clinging
like a sodden shroud

such peace
fullness
no endless chatter
distracting from the magic
of this time out of time
no frontal lobe logic
second guessing
and labeling
my world

somehow something
sweet
hypnotically fragrant
and as gentle as a shift
in the wind
on an easy summer's day

touched my soul
so that I sensed
with quiet certainty
that everything is
now and forever
all right

will it come again?
I wonder
perhaps if
only I can
stop the endless
and escalating momentum
of my questioning
"where?" and "how?" and "why?"
for now at least
there is nothing
to say except
"Thank You!"

⌘ ⌘ ⌘ ⌘ ⌘ ⌘

something in me
loves the morning
and applauds the
sun as he emerges
from his ocean bath
dripping with the
promise of a
new day

something in me
loves the late afternoon
while the day
well spent
lays at my feet
I can curl into the
softness of
its receding light

something in me
loves the evening
stars exploding overhead
announce God in
Her heaven
as I don my shawl
and slip outside
to gaze in awe
at the spectacle

something in me
loves the wee small hours
the soft black stillness
that invites me to
rest my weary self
curled into the warm
firmness of my beloved

⌘ ⌘ ⌘ ⌘ ⌘ ⌘

drowning in minutia
a swirling eddy
of duties and details
I struggle against the undertow
of obligations, offerings,
opportunities
pulling me down
and down

until somehow
brought to the depths
of overwhelm and exhaustion
I release everything
that would weigh on me
and find myself
buoyed up
and up

stripped bare
floating on the surface
gasping for breath
I surrender at last
to the gentle current
that carries my unencumbered self
to the surety and sweetness
of today's shore

perhaps next time I will remember
to travel light
⌘ ⌘ ⌘ ⌘ ⌘ ⌘

too busy too often too much
I wind up out of touch
with all that really matters
my life shred into tatters
continually distracted
my sense of self protracted
groping around in a maze
disconnected and in a daze

too often too much too busy
racing about in a tizzy
endless lists of things to do
accomplishing all too few
while life is passing by
no matter how I try
to keep up with the pace
it's just too tough a race

too much too busy too often
still there are times when I soften
and finding my still point within
open my heart and begin
to seek a clearer direction
by asking the age old questions
Who am I? Why am I here?
What do I love? What do I hold dear?

too little too seldom too rare
are these moments when I dare
to step out of the fray
searching for a simpler way
but in these brief breaths of peace
when life's tumultuous demands I release
I can feel what I've always known
that my soul can find its way home

...if I will but surrender
love what I love and be tender

⌘ ⌘ ⌘ ⌘ ⌘ ⌘

undeniable
this fierce yearning
pressing at me
from the inside

uncontainable
this awful burning
flames licking
at my illusions

irrepressible
this surging lustiness
begging release
from repressive restraints

unknowable
the joyful consequences
embedded within
the word "YES!"

immeasurable
the ecstatic possibilities
presented to those
who break through..

...and connect with life

⌘ ⌘ ⌘ ⌘ ⌘ ⌘

it is not a question
of perfection
though for years
I have struggled
against all that I am not
yet
it is not about goodness
or worthiness
though for years
I have judged myself
by some ephemeral ideal
alas
it is not simply a tallying
of accomplishments
though I sometimes measure
the worth of my days
by that illusive yardstick
still
how difficult I have made it
for life
to break through
the hardened shell
of my "cannots" and "shoulds"
but
when I listen
with great care
there is music all around

inviting me at every moment
to open my arms
and
whirl around
in the embrace
of the Beloved
to the tempo
of life's song
simply
attending to
the grace and joy and beauty
of each movement
knowing with exquisite certainty
that it's never too late
surely
nor do I have to know
all the right steps
in order
to let myself
dance

⌘ ⌘ ⌘ ⌘ ⌘ ⌘

unraveling and unfolding

reluctant am I
to awaken abruptly
while hues of darkness
still paint the sky
while dreams play
hide and seek
in the spaciousness
between my sleep world
and wake fullness

while the soft cocoon
of my warm bed
envelops me
while the firm cradle
of my true love's arms
holds me safe
the stillness feels
all too precious
to disturb disrespectfully

lingering sweetly
in my blanket
of nocturnal sanctuary
I whisper my prayers
of gratitude
and then ever so slowly

like a lazy lioness
stretch and unfold myself
into the waiting day

it has taken
a lifetime to learn
to abandon the unraveling
perpetrated
by the harsh intrusion
of my alarm sounding
and trust instead
my deep Self
to hear
the soft invitation
of morning
greeting me by name

⌘ ⌘ ⌘ ⌘ ⌘ ⌘

sometimes
it is all
just too much
too much to fathom
too much to analyze
too much to accept
too much to do

sometimes
it is better
to just let go
of all the problems
of all the tasks
of all the burdens
that weigh me down

sometimes
the greatest gift
I can give myself
is to walk away
to walk out from under
to walk into the sunshine
and to warm my soul

sometimes
when I return
my absence
has allowed for a shift
and the burdens seem
somehow easier
than before

then sometimes
I remember
to be grateful
and to rest
in the assuredness
that I am
enough after all

⌘ ⌘ ⌘ ⌘ ⌘ ⌘

life teaches me
again and again
there is only this moment
this very moment
for me to love
and create
and follow my bliss
and sing my song
to the world
and listen with gratitude
as the world
sings her song to me

life shows me
again and again
that what was true
perfectly true
just yesterday
may not be so today
nuances and paradoxes
of right and wrong
brighten and fade
shift and shimmer
playing havoc
with my desire
for absolute clarity

life reminds me
again and again
of her preciousness

and her fragility
the fruit set aside
for tomorrow
loses its crisp
freshness and rots
the moment postponed
loses its joyful spontaneity

life holds me
again and again
in her embrace
inviting me to dance
right here and now
under this moon
and these stars
with no assurances
that there will be music
or stars
tomorrow

how foolish I can be
ignoring the immediacy
of life's blessings
the temporary nature
of life's offerings
while all around me
flowers bloom and die

⌘ ⌘ ⌘ ⌘ ⌘ ⌘

ahhhh sweet slumber
the familiar descent
on cool sheets
into otherwhere
a magical ride
away
from the fullness
of today's tasks
and tumult
when I have allowed
them to overwhelm
my spirit

a proper sleep
with time for dreaming
transforms
my catalogue of concerns
into something
mystical and enigmatic
revealing
a glimpse
of faraway kingdoms
rich with possibility
awaiting my discovery

rested and renewed
I am gifted
at the far end
of this dreamtime
by a spacious entry
to a new day's dawning
across a magnificent threshold
worthy of this heroine's return
from her far journey
to the land of Nod

⌘ ⌘ ⌘ ⌘ ⌘ ⌘

to live well
and fully
I must befriend life
not as I wish it
to be
but as it is
only by dropping
my cloak of caution
can I stretch
my arms wide
enough to beckon
life
into my embrace

there is no loving life
if "when" and "then"
continually seduce me
like the Greek Sirens
away
from my true North
only to break me
apart
on their craggy shores

only by resting
my finger
on the pulse
of what is
real
and feeling
the beat
reverberate
in and through me
can I serve
life
appreciative of
the immediacy and
aliveness
of what quite simply
is

⌘ ⌘ ⌘ ⌘ ⌘ ⌘

I am womanheart
at the core
of my being
fully and
unabashedly female

I am womansoul
deep within
hips and breasts
blood and bone
my essence thrives

I am womankind
passionate
playful
open to receive
open to share

I am womanspirit
audaciously
alive
rejoicing
in connection

I am Woman

⌘ ⌘ ⌘ ⌘ ⌘ ⌘

one acorn

so many trees

one tree

so many birds

one bird

so many songs

one song

so many smiles

one smile

so many blessings

one blessing

so much love

⌘ ⌘ ⌘ ⌘ ⌘ ⌘

refreshing moments

as calming as
the space of a breath
between the comings
and goings
of my chattering mind

as touching as
the offering of a hand
to someone
who squeezes back
in return

as kind as
the gracious listener
willing to hear
beyond
my inadequate voicings

as inspiring as
the gift of love
from a sisterfriend
willing to
celebrate my dreams

as precious as
the kindness of strangers
reminding me
that we are
not separate

as sustaining as
the strong shoulder
upon which to rest
when it all just seems
too much

as gentle as
the feeling
of God's forgiveness
when I cannot forgive
myself

⌘ ⌘ ⌘ ⌘ ⌘ ⌘

CONNECTING MOMENTS

"The meeting of two personalities is like the contact of two chemical substances; if there is any reaction, both are transformed."

≈ C.G. Jung

things happen
life happens
while we plan
and plod
while we dig
and dream
while we caress
and create
the forces of life
push and pull
at our efforts

thoughts
yours and mine
and actions
mine and yours
scatter seeds
hither or yon
some take root
others decompose
becoming fertile ground
for what next

things happen
life happens
and
ours is not to reason
or rail about why
all that really matters
is this –
how we respond
to happenstance
and how we hold each other
along the way

⌘ ⌘ ⌘ ⌘ ⌘ ⌘

all it takes
is a question
any question
about peace
or passion
about hope or happiness
something anything
real
really
anything that matters
anything at all

the magic of conversation
waves a wand
and we begin
word by word
to awaken to each other
to pay attention
and to know feel sense
our common humanity
and connectedness

neither agreement
nor orderliness
is necessary
only compassion
and a willingness
to listen and share

beyond the chatter
and judgments
that would distract
and disconnect us

with only hand on heart
truthfulness
and an open space
to receive it
we could
I am sure
change the world
don't you agree?
and
if so
talk with me
please
just talk with me

⌘ ⌘ ⌘ ⌘ ⌘ ⌘

I know you.
Haven't I always known you?
cellular memories
from somewhere
deep inside
push up and through
today's amorphous reality
revealing a primal bond
awakened by your presence

You know me.
Haven't you always known me?
this connection
so deep and familiar
binding us
soul to soul
must have had its birth
in time before time
how magnificent
to have found you again

⌘ ⌘ ⌘ ⌘ ⌘ ⌘

forgiveness

as long as I carve
my anger in stone
as long as I keep
a tally of injustices
as long as I fill
my ledger with small deceits
as long as I seek
retribution and rebuttal
as long as I justify my failures
and rationalize my inertia
there can be no peace

perhaps that is why
the gift of forgiveness
is so precious
perhaps that is why
it is so very foolish
to believe that
by offering my pardon
to others
for perceived wrongs
I am giving them
a great gift
while all the while
it is I who am
the great beneficiary
of such graciousness
⌘ ⌘ ⌘ ⌘ ⌘ ⌘

please dear friend
do not judge me
through your fears
or fantasies
holding up
your good ideas
of right and wrong
as irrefutable
or immutable

I do not mean to hurt you
but there is more
so much more
to know and understand
the rich ambiguity
of truth
lies in its paradoxes
such is the blessing
and challenge of life

I now know that
sometimes
to honor one's Self
one must disappoint another
and sometimes
to embrace one possibility
one risks denying
another

and so it is
that choices
pull at our souls
forcing us
again and again
to be true to ourselves
at any cost

⌘ ⌘ ⌘ ⌘ ⌘ ⌘

I am more
so much more
than I have shown you
shyness or reluctance
veil the vastness
of my heart
logic and caution
serve as censors
to the meanderings
of my mind

concealed
is the fullness
of my capacity for joy
hidden is the depth
of my hunger for connection
I am
as infinite as the All
from which I come

my soul dances
at the edge
of your awareness
wanting to expose
her Self
in all her paradoxical splendor
but I am more
so much more
than you are willing to see
⌘ ⌘ ⌘ ⌘ ⌘ ⌘

I have included the following two poems, chosen from many I wrote in the aftermath of 9/11/02, because they speak to the power of connection.

innocent
we were
once
upon a time
and arrogant
building
towers that
could touch
the sky
almost
with nary
a thought
of how tempting
it would be
to knock them
down

child's play
building blocks
toppled
in a moment
dreams crushed

under a mountain
of rubble
while
we who survive
breathe in the dust
and hear the cries
of those
lost
in the crumbled remains
along with our illusions
of invincibility

amazing
how everything
insubstantial
falls away
in the wake of disaster

falling towers
implode on
our small worries
and wants
burying with them
our naïveté
and our selfishness

rising
from the ash covered debacle
with resolve
and courage
our Phoenix-Self
stretches out
to embrace
that which is essential -
compassion
connection
charity
faith
hope

oh world
hear our cries
not just the agony
of our collective pain
but our plea
for unity
against all that would destroy
the human capacity
for kindness and love
and
the will and power
to be just

⌘ ⌘ ⌘ ⌘ ⌘ ⌘

shocked
shaken
terrified
we watched
our world
crash and burn
as we gasped
and suffocated from
the explosive air
blinded by the dust
not knowing
what to do
or say
or believe

yet somehow
we groped about
knowing enough
to find one another
and to come together
so that our hearts might heal
our courage grow
and our hope be restored
in the sanctuary
of community

we gathered
together in our humanness
and frailty
keeping vigil
in each other's homes
and on corners everywhere
around the globe
with candles burning
we began again
to light the world
with our love

⌘ ⌘ ⌘ ⌘ ⌘ ⌘

just here
   just now
      justice
         but whose?
            my good idea
               or yours?
                  but not theirs?
                     or theirs which
                          makes a mockery
                              of ours?

such
   a simple idea
      justice
         is just
            the beginning of
               endless soul searching
                  inquiries with no
                     right answer
                        or righteous way

and yet
it matters
everything matters
and that we must try
to respond justly
to all life
in the moment
as best we can
with willing hearts
just is
what's true

⌘ ⌘ ⌘ ⌘ ⌘ ⌘

the women's circle

facing each other
a circle is formed
our breath merges
at the center
connecting us
and inspiring
our union

gracefully arranged
upon an altar
we lay sacred talismans
offering
intimate glimpses
of each soul's journey
to this point in time

prayers are uttered
to bless our gathering
as we begin
the process
of hearing each other
and ourselves
into wholeness

⌘ ⌘ ⌘ ⌘ ⌘ ⌘

Ubuntu

"Ubuntu - I am because you are, you are because I am...." is a deep African way of being.
A teaching from _The Book of Awakening_
by poet and philosopher Mark Nepo

"I miss my breast"
my friend whispers
her grief
into the air
like spring rain
her words
fall softly
all around us

"of course you do
how could you not
how courageous of you
to speak such truth
without adornment
and how blessed am I
to receive
your words"

"Ubuntu! Ubuntu!"
I hold her
and we weep
"my grief is yours
your grief is mine"

"ubuntu! ubuntu!"
she holds me
and we sigh
"your truth is mine
my truth is yours"

"I miss my breast"
my friend screams
her rage
into the world
like thunder
her words
echo through
the chasms of life

"of course you do
as do we your sisters
across time and space
how could we not
we who have sacrificed
our bosoms
on the altar of hope
in a bargain for our lives"

"ubuntu! ubuntu!"
ancient voices join
in agreement
"your pain is mine
my pain is yours"

"ubuntu! ubuntu!"
they chorus
in harmony
"my journey is yours
your journey is mine"

"I miss my breast"
my friend speaks
her acceptance
into the air
like a pipe of peace
her surrender
sending prayers of love
to all that is... and will yet be

"of course you do
as we will miss
your nurturing milk
but we will suckle instead
at the breast
of your compassion
and your strength
and your wisdom"

"ubuntu! ubuntu!"
sing the yet unborn
to this sistermotherfriend
"my future is yours
your past is mine"

"Ubuntu! Ubuntu!"
women everywhere
standing side by side
"my story is yours
your story is mine"

"we are one
we are one
ubuntu!
ubuntu!
I am you
I am you
ubuntu!"

❆ ❆ ❆ ❆ ❆ ❆

invisible kindnesses

more and more it is
the small things
that touch my soul and
awaken me to
the awe
of your humanity
and my own

the news of the day
when I can bear to
watch or listen
offers detailed dramas
magnified images
of war and greed
intolerance and grief

they pierce my soul
leaving me
empty
and discouraged
desperate to break
through the bonds
of my impotence

but in a camp of
festering evil
my uncle a boy of 14
would offer his daily bread
to another
whose hunger
could not be assuaged

and
in a town
years and miles away
my great grandmother
lovingly
suckled the babe
of another
too sick to care

elsewhere still
children labeled
feeble-minded
turned away from the finish
line and victory
to comfort
one of their own who
had fallen in the race

invisible kindnesses
sprinkled like manna
everywhere offer
sustenance when
my panoramic planetary
view would leave me
blinded and terrified
immobilized by dismay

like a flower
that blooms against
all odds
in the crack of
the prison wall
I too can turn my face
to a sliver of light

and find
what I need
to sustain my soul
and summon the
courage to offer
my own invisible gesture
to the world

⌘ ⌘ ⌘ ⌘ ⌘ ⌘

the wedding day

it is of course
a most joyous time
vows and kisses
offered and received
hearts flung wide
open
to this new promise
of forever

but forever
is made of days
each one
precious and unique
each one
a stepping stone
to who knows what
lies ahead
each one
a microcosm
of the complexity
of life

and so
as one who has
day by day
for almost 35 years
lived within the confines
and shelter of
this long embrace
I offer you
as a gift
one thought
for the journey

simply this
honor your own
and each other's wholeness
fully rather than selectively
as you offer each other
a generosity of space
in which to grow
and a wellspring of love
from which to draw sustenance

written for the occasion of my son Reid's marriage to Susie
October 2002

⌘ ⌘ ⌘ ⌘ ⌘ ⌘

to my husband on the occasion of
our 35th wedding anniversary

familiar rhythms
well worn patterns
on sheets
that know us
have felt our
intertwinings
and witnessed
our release
again and again
creaky coils
lending music
to this dance
we've danced
for a lifetime
together
accommodating
each nuance
and shift
that accompanies
us
as we grow older
together

⌘ ⌘ ⌘ ⌘ ⌘ ⌘

the gift of being enough

in this world
of not enoughness
where there is always
something more to do
something more to become
your great gift to me
is seeing myself
reflected in your eyes
where loving acceptance
shines a holy light
upon my soul

in this world
of more is better
where there is always
something more to possess
something more to achieve
may my great gift to you
be that you feel me always
holding you
in all your imperfect splendor
with abundant gratitude
for your presence
in my life

in this world
of constant striving
where there appears to always be
someone more worthy
someone more perfect
may our great gift to each other
be that we embrace
again and again
our divinity
yours and mine
as we hold one another
with hands
and heart
as we celebrate
the gifts we are

in this world

in this world

⌘ ⌘ ⌘ ⌘ ⌘ ⌘

The Gift of a Poem

there are poems
everywhere
playing among the stars
and lying in the grass
in the old man's walk
and the child's delight
poets have found them
along the ocean's edge
and deep in the wilderness
amidst the city's cacophonous cries
and in the wind's whisper
at the edge of the world

sometimes
I find them
lucky me
beneath my pillow
other times they
hide beneath stones
waiting for my restless
foot to kick them
free
sometimes
it seems
they have disappeared forever

and no amount
of cajoling or candle lighting
will coax them out of hiding

then
just as I have surrendered
to their silence
they shout
SURPRISE
and words fall
like confetti
everywhere
in a celebration
of colorful profusion
while I race about
gathering them in

⌘ ⌘ ⌘ ⌘ ⌘ ⌘

Thank you, dear reader, for spending time with all that I have gathered here. By doing so you have touched my soul. My hope is that I have touched yours as well.

Blessings,

Minx

July 13th, 2003

About the Author

Here I am 50 plus and still looking for ways to creatively expand my horizons. I love lighthearted laughter, deep self-discovery, and conversations that can change the world. As a *certified personal and business coach* and founder of Fourfold Path Inc. I am committed to journeying with clients on a fourfold path - *physical, mental, emotional, & spiritual* – toward greater integrity and joy. As co-founder, with Marsha Lehman, of Authentic Woman Enterprises LLC, I am dedicated to creating opportunities for women to tap into their authenticity through the power and poignancy of true connection. We are co-authors of a number of playbooks, playshops, and facilitated conversations including *THE PJ PARTY RETREAT, FRESH START, THE MENOPOWER® HOUR,* and *X-RATED SELF-CARE* as well as co-authors of <u>Hold Me – A More Than Coloring Book</u>, <u>The Inner Coach® Series</u>, and <u>The PJ Party Retreat Book – Women Really Love to Have Fun</u>.

For more information or to order books & CDs, please e-mail <u>minx@coachminx.com</u> and visit me on the web at <u>www.CoachMinx.com</u> and <u>www.AuthenticWoman.com</u>.

What readers have to say...

I have just read your poems and I am gasping for breath... for real. You have spilled your guts and come up refreshed and clean. Bravo!

≈ Florence Ross, Ph.D.

Authenticity and vulnerability of a woman writing from her own experience and perceptions of the world around her is what makes Minx's poetry such a gift to anyone who journeys through it.

≈ Deborah Roth, MA

Speaking of messages, those that you have so poetically penned from the heart are both deep and revealing. This seemingly simple work is not only well crafted, but also courageous.

≈ Dr. Gary Wiren

As for your poems, they touch the very core of what it is to be human. I thank you for it.

≈ Leslee Landau

You my fair Lady of Poetic Genius are the microcosm of Galatia, Gaea, The Great Matriarch, Earth Mother---keeper of love, life, and records. I love your Great Gift.

≈ Don Tolman